St. Francis School
Library

DATE DUE

Hummingbirds

ABDO Publishing Company

A Buddy Book
by
Julie Murray

VISIT US AT
www.abdopub.com

Published by Buddy Books, an imprint of ABDO Publishing Company, 4940 Viking Drive, Suite 622, Edina, Minnesota 55435. Copyright © 2005 by Abdo Consulting Group, Inc. International copyrights reserved in all countries. No part of this book may be reproduced in any form without written permission from the publisher.

Printed in the United States.

Edited by: Christy DeVillier
Contributing Editors: Matt Ray, Michael P. Goecke
Graphic Design: Maria Hosley
Image Research: Deborah Coldiron
Photographs: Corel, Minden Pictures

Library of Congress Cataloging-in-Publication Data

Murray, Julie, 1969-
    Hummingbirds/Julie Murray.
        p. cm. — (Animal kingdom. Set II)
    Includes bibliographical references and index.
    Contents: Birds — Hummingbirds — Size and color — Amazing flyers — What they eat — Where they live — Their nests — Babies — Backyard hummingbirds.
    ISBN 1-59197-320-1
        1. Hummingbirds—Juvenile literature. [1. Hummingbirds.] I. Title.

QL696.A558M86 2003
598.7'64—dc21

2003041948

Contents

Hummingbirds 4

What They Look Like 6

Where They Live 10

Flying 14

Eating 16

Nests 18

Hummingbird Chicks 20

Important Words 23

Web Sites 23

Index 24

Hummingbirds

Birds live all around the world. There are more than 9,000 kinds of birds. All birds have wings and feathers. They have beaks and no teeth.

There are more than 300 kinds of hummingbirds. Most hummingbirds are tiny and colorful. They are famous for their flying skills.

The smallest bird in the world is a hummingbird.

What They Look Like

The smallest bird in the world is the bee hummingbird. It grows to become about two inches (five cm) long. Most adult hummingbirds are between three and five inches (8 and 13 cm) long.

The largest hummingbird is the giant hummingbird. Adults are about eight inches (20 cm) long.

Some hummingbirds have many bright colors. They may have green, blue, red, or purple feathers. Male hummingbirds are more colorful than females. Males commonly have a brightly colored throat. This is called a **gorget**.

This male hummingbird has a purple gorget.

Where They Live

Hummingbirds live in North America and South America. They live in deserts, **tropical** forests, mountains, valleys, and grasslands. Most hummingbirds live in warm places where flowers bloom all year.

This hummingbird lives in a rain forest in Costa Rica.

Some hummingbirds live in places that have cold winters. These hummingbirds travel south for the winter. This is called **migrating**.

The rufous hummingbird migrates far each fall. It flies about 2,500 miles (4,023 km) from Alaska to Mexico.

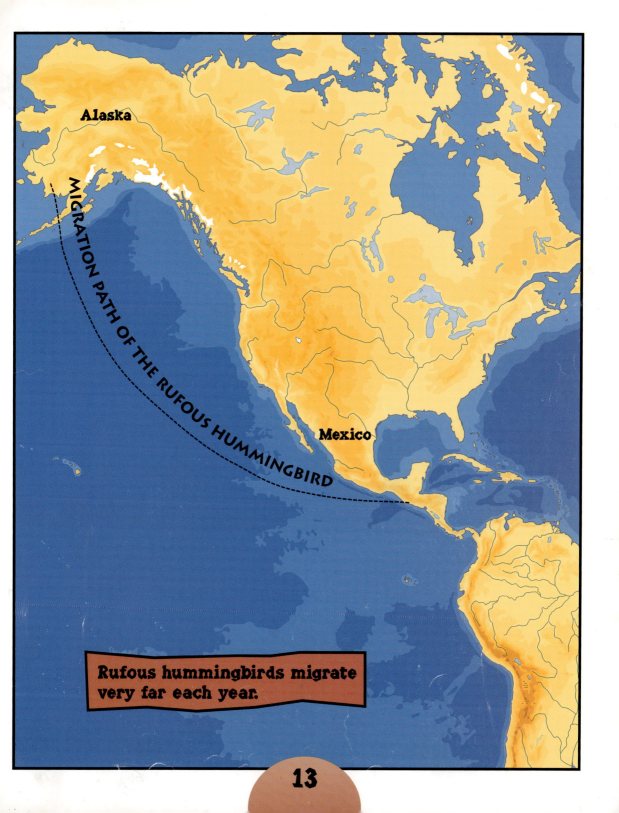

Flying

Hummingbirds can fly about 25 miles (40 km) per hour. They can fly straight up, straight down, or backward. Hummingbirds can also **hover** in the air.

Hummingbirds can fly in many directions.

Hummingbirds can hover in one place as they eat.

Hummingbirds flap their wings very fast. They can flap them 70 times in one second. Their flapping wings make a humming sound. This is why people call them hummingbirds.

Eating

Hummingbirds eat small insects. They also visit flowers in search of **nectar**. Nectar is a sweet liquid that some plants make. Hummingbirds use their long, thin beaks to reach the nectar. They drink it up very fast.

Drinking flower nectar helps hummingbirds fly fast.

Feeding Hummingbirds

Hummingbirds live in backyards across the United States. People enjoy feeding these backyard birds. They fill special hummingbird feeders with sugar water. Hummingbirds enjoy drinking the sugar water. They will go to a feeder many times a day.

Nests

Hummingbirds build nests in the spring. They build nests with grass, leaves, and other plant parts. Hummingbirds use spider webs, too. Building a nest may take five days or more. It is very small.

A hummingbird in its nest.

Hummingbird Chicks

A female hummingbird lays two eggs at a time. The eggs are less than one inch (three cm) long. She sits on the eggs to keep them warm. This is called **incubation**.

After 14 days, the eggs hatch. The newly hatched chicks are blind and featherless. They are the size of a small bee.

A mother hummingbird and her chicks.

The mother hummingbird feeds her chicks. After three or four weeks, they can fly. Most hummingbirds live only a few years.

Hummingbirds leave the family nest after they are fully grown.

Important Words

gorget the brightly colored throat area on a male hummingbird.

hover to stay in the air near one place.

incubation keeping eggs warm before they hatch.

migrate to move from one place to another when the seasons change.

nectar the sweet liquid, or sugar water, that flowers make.

tropical warm and wet weather.

Web Sites

To learn more about hummingbirds, visit ABDO Publishing Company on the World Wide Web. Web sites about hummingbirds are featured on our Book Links page. These links are routinely monitored and updated to provide the most current information available.

www.abdopub.com

Index

Alaska **12, 13**

beaks **4, 16**

bee hummingbirds **6, 7**

chicks **20, 21, 22**

Costa Rica **11**

eggs **20**

feathers **4, 8, 20**

female hummingbirds **8, 20**

flowers **10, 16**

giant hummingbirds **6, 7**

gorget **8, 9**

hover **14, 15**

hummingbird feeders **17**

incubation **20**

insects **16**

male hummingbirds **8, 9**

Mexico **12, 13**

migrate **12, 13**

nectar **16**

nests **18, 19, 22**

North America **10**

rufous hummingbirds **12, 13**

South America **10**

United States **17**

wings **4, 15**